Budgerigars or Parakeet as Pets

A Complete Pet Guide

Parakeet or Budgerigar Facts & Information, where to buy, health, diet, lifespan, types, breeding, fun facts and more!

By Lolly Brown

Copyrights and Trademarks

Disclaimer and Legal Notice

Foreword

Budgerigars have been around long before humans! These birds ancestors' stretched back for millennia and had been kept as pets since the 1800's!

Budgerigar parrots were admired by bird enthusiasts because of their outgoing personalities and vibrant appearance. Many pet owners believe that with "budgies" there's a lot more than meets the eye!

Although Budgerigars are truly a great choice as pets, these birds doesn't come with a thin instruction manual. But fear not! In this book you'll be easily guided on understanding your Budgerigars, their nature, their behavior and characteristics, how you should feed and care for them and a whole lot more.

Embark on a wonderful journey of sharing your life with a Budgerigar Parrot. Learn to maximize the great privilege of living with one and be able to share this unique and unforgettable experience just like the many pet owners that came before you!

Table of Contents

Chapter One: Introduction

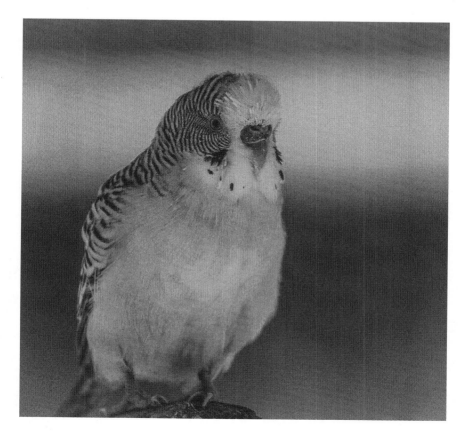

The name, "budgerigar" came from the root word "budgery" which means good bird! Budgerigars have a reputation for being small but incredible! Its vibrant appearance goes along with its enthusiastic attitude, and that's what kept these birds unique throughout the ages!

Aside from its attractive and beautiful array of colors and mutations, just like other birds, budgies also have an outgoing personality and they are very inquisitive in nature. They are very fond of playing and hanging around people and they love to yawn, which you may find yourself doing too, if you saw them do it!

They are a type of parakeets that are classified under the genus of *Melopsittacus;* these birds are scientifically known as *Melopsittacus Undulates.* Later on in this book, you will learn more about the different colors and mutations of Budgerigar parrots so that you can choose what is best for you!

Budgerigars are great as pets, though sometimes some people may find its attitude naughty because of its natural curiosity and could be way interactive at times, but that's of course, part of who they are. They are clever and can be easily trained and they can sing as well! Although, Budgerigars are generally easy to care for because of its small size, you will still need some useful tips, so that you can maximize its true potential.

Compare to other bird species, Budgerigar parrots doesn't live for 50 years or more. These birds have an average lifespan of only 15 - 20 years! But, if you take good care of them, they will certainly live longer than you might expect. They're friendly and charming companions, and because of that you need some guidance on how to take care of them, raise them and possibly learn how to be like them as well as teach them to be like you!!

Fortunately, this ultimate guide will teach you on how to be the best Budgerigar owner you can be! Inside this book, you will find tons of helpful information about Budgerigar Parrots: how they live, how to deal with them and realize the great benefits of owning one!

Glossary of Important Terms

Abdomen - bottom part of the bird

Alula - three feathers springing from the base of the primaries

Axillary - ventral area between the body and the wing

Birdhouse - another name for a nest box, or a home for a bird

Blood Feather - any feather which still has a blood supply to it

Breast - front part of the chest

Breast band - stripe across the breast

Breast spot - small, differently colored area on the breast

Breeding Cycle - time period beginning at nest building through egg laying and raising young to the point of independence

Breeding Plumage - referring to the colorful plumage which the males of many species acquire for the breeding season

Brood - young of a bird that are hatched or cared for at one time

Carnivorous - flesh-eating birds

Cap - top of the crown

Cere - fleshy area between the beak and face

Cheek - area of head below eye and above the neck

Chest - front part of the body

Scapulars - area of feathers between the back and the wings

Secondaries - flight feathers attached to the "elbow"

Secondary coverts - feathers protecting and covering the secondaries

Shoulder - feathers overlying bases of median secondary coverts

Side - area between the belly and the wing

Spectacle - eye ring and supraloral line together.

Speculum - highly colored area on secondaries of several ducks.

Subterminal band - stripe before tip of tail.

Tail - feathers extending from the rear of the bird.

Tail coverts - under and upper tail coverts.

Tarsus - part of the leg between the knee and the foot.

Taxonomy - the way bird scientists classify bird species based on their similarities to or difference s from one another

Terminal band - stripe at tip of tail

Tertiaries - feathers adjoining the secondaries

Throat - front part of the neck

Throat patch - front part of the neck

Tibia - part of the leg above the knee

Underparts - belly, undertail coverts, chest, flanks, and fore neck

Undertail coverts - feathers covering underside of base of tail

Underwing - underside of wing

Upper mandible - upper part of the bill

Upperparts - back, rump, hindneck, wings, and crown

Uppertail coverts - feathers covering upperside of base of tail

Upperwing - upperside of wing

Weaned Bird - a bird that is out of the nest, and eating on its own

Whisker - area at the sides of the chin

Wing bars - pale tips of secondary coverts creating a stripe on wings

Wing coverlets - primary and secondary coverts, or feathers overlaying others

Wing lining - median, lesser and marginal coverts on underwing

Wingspread - distance from tip to tip of the longest primary feathers of the outstretched wings

Wing stripe - paler area at base of flight feathers

Wing pit - between the body and the wing

Wrist - area at base of the primaries

Zoonosis - a zoonosis is any disease of animals that can be contracted by a human being

Chapter Two: Meet Budgerigars

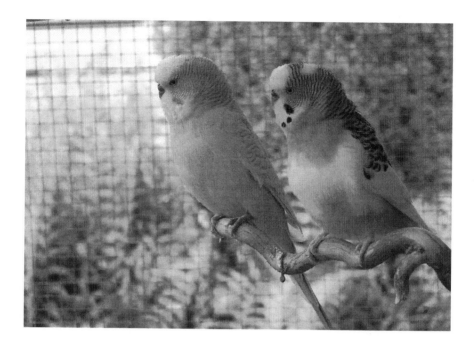

Budgerigars, also known as "common pet parakeet" or "shell parakeet" and often referred to as "the budgie," are very enchanting birds to care for and very low maintenance at the same time. These birds are also considered as one of the most underrated parakeet. Budgerigars are very ideal pets especially for first time bird owners. But before getting a fascinating parrot as your pet, it's very important that you know what it is inside out! Like many other things, you need to have proper knowledge and invest a significant amount of time to truly study and understand where these birds are coming from. That is how you will determine if this kind of pet is the right choice, so that you know what you are dealing with.

On the next sections, you'll be introduced to the friendliest and one of the most low profile parrots in the world. Prepare to meet Budgerigars!

Facts about Budgerigars

Budgerigars, which are scientifically under the Subfamily of *Loriinae*, are birds that are native to the wild and drier parts Australia. These birds life expectancy is about 15 – 20 years or more!

They are relatively small parakeets with an enthusiastic, sociable attitude towards people, which makes them an interesting choice as pets.

These parrots had been popular since the 19th century especially when scientists brought it to Europe.

In the wild, Budgerigars are miniature birds with variety of colorful feathers such as green with yellow, with black stripes and markings, and dark blue-green-black flight and tail feathers, and because of color mutations they now come in an array of different jelly bean colors like yellow, white, violet, gray, sky blue, cobalt, mauve except red and pink.

Aside from talking, they are also fond of chewing, napping and playing interesting games to keep them from being bored and also to satisfy their curious minds. They are totally cool and have a knack for a fun time!

Most Budgerigars are generally easy to train and can be well-behaved as long as you provide them with adequate attention, interaction, and love. They can easily become part of the family and a loving companion if you are willing to put in the time and effort to take care of them.

Budgerigars can be quite tricky to differentiate because they have very similar appearance to the other parakeets. They display small, iridescent blue-violet cheek patches, with a light green body color. Their wings have greenish-black flight feathers and their beaks do not protrude much.

Their average size including tails is about 7 inches long, with a wingspan of about 10 – 14 inches, and weighs 30 – 40 grams. It has an average lifespan of 15 – 20 years. The maximum recorded lifespan of a budgie is 26 years although sometimes, it only lives for a minimum of 5 – 10 years.

In terms of their behavior and personality, they are quite notorious for having sharp screeching noise and bold attitude in everything. They will destroy and chew on any objects available, requires lots of interaction and at times nippy to unfamiliar faces. But they are primarily easy to tame and very friendly once they get to know you.

These parrots are omnivorous and usually feed on seeds, insects, fruit and nuts. Budgerigars are sexually dimorphic; female budgies are have white or light-blue, tan, or brown cere (head) while males commonly have blue or purplish-blue cere except for color mutated species.

In terms of reproduction, Budgerigars reach their sexual maturity as early as 6 months old and breeding period usually occurs between June and September; females' clutch size ranges from an average of 4 – 6 eggs and incubation lasts for about 18 – 21 days.

Just like any parrots, Budgerigars can be trained to mimic human speech and imitate other sounds by using their bifurcated trachea, which are equivalent to vocal cords in humans. Male budgies are usually the one who sings especially when courting.

Quick Facts

- Taxonomy: phylum *Chordata*, class *Aves*, order *Psittaciformes*, family *Psittaculidae*, Subfamily *Loriinae*, Tribe *Melopsittacini*
- **Distribution**: Australia
- **Habitat**: Scrublands, Woodlands, Grasslands
- **Lifestyle**: Flock Oriented
- **Anatomical Adaptations**:
- **Breeding Season**: between June to September
- **Eggs**: 4 – 6 eggs
- **Incubation Period**: 18 – 21 days
- **Sexual Maturity** : 6 – 7 months old
- **Average Size**: 18 cm (7 in)
- **Average Weight**: 30 – 40 grams
- **Wingspan**: 25 – 36 cm (10 – 14 in)
- **Coloration**: (in the wild) yellow, white, violet, gray, sky blue, cobalt, mauve; over 100 color mutations
- **Sexual Dimorphism**: Sexually dimorphic
- **Diet**: Seeds, Insects, Fruit, Nuts (Omnivore)
- **Sounds**: Vocal Communicator
- **Interaction**: Highly Social
- **Lifespan**: 15 – 20 years

Budgerigars in History

Budgies are native to Australia, and the first humans who came into contact with them over thousands of years ago were most likely the aborigines of that land.

In 1805, an English zoologist and botanist named George Shaw made the first ever recorded description of the budgerigar.

In 1840, an English ornithologist named John Gould, brought to Europe the first budgerigar, where it was admired by a lot of European bird enthusiasts and just a decade later, during the 1850s the first captive breeding began.

In 1870's, the first recorded color variation was made, and a wide variety of color mutated budgies followed shortly thereafter.

During the 20th century, the budgerigar's popularity as a family pet rose dramatically and began importation in United States, South America and Asia.

Today, the bird continues to be a very popular pet because it's very low maintenance, perfect for families with children and a very gorgeous cute companion that you can count on.

Color Mutations of Budgerigars

Unlike other parakeets, Budgerigars doesn't have any other sub-species, but it has hundreds and if not thousands of budgie color mutations and counting! Making it probably the most "color-coded" bird species in the world! There are a lot of breeders and bird enthusiasts who at one point or another, tried to create different color mutations which make a budgie very unique. These birds are available in different colors, that even as a first time pet owner like you or someone who had pet birds before can still be overwhelmed by the variety of mutations these species have!

Below are some of the basic and most popular color mutations of a Budgerigar, you can use this as reference if you're planning to buy a budgie but don't know what color to pick or it can also help you to create your own color mutation in the future! Who knows? You could come across something much more unique and beautiful with these birds!

2 Basic Varieties of Budgerigars

The base color in Budgerigars is usually shown in the mask and face feathers. It can also be found through a pearled pattern on the wings, and some stripes on the neck area.

- **Yellow-based Pigment** - All budgies have a shade of blue in their feathers, so when a budgie has a yellow pigment base the blue reflects against the yellow, which results in a normal green budgie color.
- **White-based** - it is a pigment based that lacks the yellow color. If the budgie is white-based, their blue feather has no yellow color to reflect on thus, the budgie remains blue.

Important Note:
- If your budgie has no blue colored feathers and they are yellow-based, the result is called a "Lutino budgie." It is a full-colored yellow budgie with red eyes.
- If your budgie has no blue colored feathers and they are white-based budgie, the result is called an "Albino budgie."

Dark Factors

Dark Factor ranges from zero level to one and two levels. All domestic budgies have a dark factor (except a normal green budgie)

- Dark Factor Level One (for green budgies) – it usually appears darker than a normal one. This darker green mutation is therefore called "Dark Green"
- Dark Factor Level Two (blue budgies) - it usually appears as a dark greyish-bluish color

Important Note:
- The number of DF (Dark Factors) in the parents counts in the chicks.

Grey Factor

A Grey Factor (GF) is a factor that adds grey to the normal and dominant body color.
- Green Budgies (with a DF and GF) – these birds will have a very dark – greenish – greyish appearance
- White – based Budgies (with a GF) – these birds will have some added grey – color on their feathers

Important Note:
Grey Factor is a very dominant and strong factor, which is why even the slightest gene of this factor will likely appear in budgies.

Violet Factor

The Violet Factor (VF) is also a color adding factor, just like the Grey Factor, however the VF is not as strong as the GF.

So if for instance your budgie has a VF, it may or may not show. The VF is not common in yellow-based budgies, and even if it does show up in yellow – pigment based budgies, it will likely appear as a darker green color.

- Cobalt Budgies – these birds are white-based budgies that has a Dark Factor Level One with a Violet Factor

Important Note:

Even if your budgie does not show the VF, they may show a little tinting or shade of the color at the vent, where waste and eggs are deposited during breeding process, and feet area, a great example are Muave-colored budgies, but it is still difficult to determine if they do have the Violet Factor or not.

Dilution Degree

Dilution degree is a degree measuring how much the body color of a bird is washed out; just like the Dark Factor almost all budgies have a dilution degree.

Dilution degree only means that any markings your budgie may have (stripes and pearls on neck and back, etc.) are either lighter than usual, or so light that they may even be difficult to recognize. As an example, the body color of a full Dilute budgie is washed out about 80%.

Yellow Face

Yellow-faced budgies are like in-between combination of white-based budgies and yellow-based budgies.

2 Main Types of Yellow - Face:

- Type A – are budgies with a yellow mask and may also have a little shade of yellow in his/her tail feathers.
- Type B – are budgies that are just the same appearance of type A.

The difference between the two types is that Type B turns more greenish, after the first molt and Type A stays the same, but also has a shade of sky blue.

Important Note:

Genetics for this mutation are quite hard and they are difficult to find, but ornithologists and bird enthusiasts are still trying to create this kind of mutation.

Opaline

Opaline is a mutation that makes the main body color show up on the feathers in the patterns on the budgies neck and back. This mutation has no effect to color what-so-ever.

The Opaline mutation also makes the bars normally on a budgies head thinner, which leaves more color to show through.

Spangle

Spangle is mutation that is highly similar to the Opaline mutation. It is another pattern-changing mutation, but instead of a pattern on the head/neck, it usually appears on the back and the budgies' wings. However, the Spangle mutation does not have any color spreading through the patterns like the Opaline. The pearled patterns and stripes become much thinner, causing the basic color underneath to show.

Important Note:

A budgie can be both Spangle and Opaline mutated birds! This combination has quite beautiful effects and you're very lucky if your budgie has that characteristic, its one-of-a-kind.

Cinnamon

Cinnamon is a much simpler pattern-changing mutation. But unlike the Spangle and Opaline, the Cinnamon mutation changes the color of the markings on head, neck, back, and wings to a cinnamon color.

It is very uncommon but still the basic body color budgies might gain a cinnamon tinge to it! And although it is a simple mutation, it is quite exotic and attractive!

Chapter Three: Budgerigar's Requirements

Are you now thinking of getting a Budgerigars? No problem! After learning what Budgerigars are, where they come from, how they live and its different types, it's time to give you practical tips on what you need to know before buying one.

In this chapter, you will get a whole lot of information on its pros and cons, its average monthly costs as well as the things you need so that you will be well on your way to becoming a legitimate Budgerigars pet owner -should you decide to be one! It's up to you! Read on!

Pros and Cons of Budgerigars

The information listed below is the advantages and disadvantages of owning Budgerigars:

Pros

- **Personality:** They are playful, lively and bold
- **Appearance:** Vibrant and vividly colorful with about a hundred color mutations available
- **Abilities:** Very easily trained and can sing and speak
- **Cost:** They very inexpensive and low maintenance
- **Impact on Humans:** They are very intelligent, down-to-earth and loves to interact with people; great long-time companions

Cons

- **Noise:** They are sometimes too talkative to people
- **Damage to Your Home:** They love to chew up and destroy your wooden furniture if left out of the cage
- **Behavior:** They are oftentimes lazy compared to other birds
- **Speaking Ability:** Not that good in speaking but can be trained, although male budgies can sing!

Budgerigars Behavior with Other Pets

There is actually no general rule when introducing your pet parrot with other types or species of birds, sometimes they'll get along, sometimes they won't.

Fortunately, Budgerigars in general are very welcoming to other species regardless of its kind! They are very friendly parrots, and you as the owner don't have to worry if ever you would introduce them to other birds or pets, they love to hang out with everyone including people!

There is however a flipside, Budgies tend to be harmful companions for smaller birds or birds of the same size, such as cockatiels. Even if your budgie gets along with a larger or smaller bird, accidental injuries can occur during play or when they are just simply spending time inside the cage. They are indeed, small but sometimes terrible birds so keep a tight watch over them especially if you just introduced them or if they interact with other species.

It is also best to socialize your Budgerigar while they are still young, because they are still vulnerable and can be very accepting of other members once they get used to it.

As a general rule, you can introduce other types of birds but do so with caution so that they could easily warm up with their new feathered friends.

Unlike other birds that are highly individual, Budgerigars love to be in flocks when they're in the wild or even in captivity. It'll be easy to train them to like other parrots, though sometimes they can be a bit witty.

Experts also suggest that the best behaved Budgerigars are those who were exposed to lots of change in the environment and the ones who were trained to socialize with people, because they become more adjusted.

Ease and Cost of Care

Owning a Budgerigars parrot is very inexpensive and keeping one is also very low maintenance, since they are small birds. However, the supplies needed in keeping one will definitely add up to your daily life expenses, if you want to keep a Budgerigars as a pet you should be able to cover the necessary costs it entails.

In this section you will receive an overview of the expenses associated with purchasing and keeping a Budgerigar as a pet.

Initial Costs

The initial expenses associated with keeping Budgerigar as pets include the cost of the bird itself as well as the cage, cage accessories, toys, and grooming supplies.

You will find an overview of these costs below as well as the estimated total expense for keeping a Budgerigar:

Purchase Price: starts at $10 - $100

As established earlier Budgerigars are miniatures in size, very common and not hard to find, that's why these birds are the cheapest parakeets among the cheapest parakeets in the world! However, it also depends on the color of the bird; some Budgerigar with rare color mutations or is a show quality of breed could be more expensive than others.

The general rules in these birds are, the more colorful, rarer and clever it is, the more expensive it can be. So better check your budget to see which Budgerigar is best for you.
Cage: starts at $59 - $400

The bigger, the better! Even if your Budgerigars are small, it's a general rule for birds that they live in cages where they could have the luxury of space, after all that is where they're going to spend most of their time right? So pick the right cage for your Budgerigars, so that they'll enjoy life like you!

Accessories: estimated $100 in total

If you bought a cage, you'll definitely need cage accessories like perches, lights, feeding dishes, stands, cage covers and harnesses for your Budgerigars. Accessories can be quite expensive depending on the brand as well as the quality and size of your purchase. Budgerigars are like other birds have a naughty side too, they'll chew everything! Watch out!

Toys: more or less $50 in total

Budgerigars love to play and chew lots of toys! They will easily destroy any toy that came there way, which usually means that you may need to keep buying more often. Like other parrots, they need plenty of stimulation to keep their intelligent and curious minds entertained. The price of the toys depends on the brand you choose to buy. Keep birdie boredom at bay with chewable toys for your Budgerigar.

Grooming Supplies: more or less $50 in total

As part of pet hygiene, your feathered friend needs to be cleaned and properly groomed. There are lots of grooming supplies that you can buy online or in your local pet store. Again, the brand and quality of the product affect the price range to keep your Budgerigars clean and healthy.

Initial Cost for Budgerigars	
Cost Type	**Approximate Cost**
Purchase Price	$10 - $100 (£7.52 - £75.22)
Cage	$59 - $400 (£44.38 - £300.88)
Accessories	$100 (£75.22)
Toys	$50 (£37.61)
Grooming Supplies	$50 (£37.61)
Total	$269 - $700 (£202.34 - £526.53)

*Please note that these amounts are computed at the starting price and converted at the current exchange rate, which is $1 = £0.75.

Costs may vary.

Monthly Costs

The monthly costs associated with keeping a Budgerigar can be quite expensive even if they are generally low maintenance. Some of the things that needs to be bought on a monthly basis like food supplements, cleaning materials and even veterinary care every now and then will definitely add up to your expenses. Below are the estimate monthly costs it entails.

Bird Food (seeds, pellets, treats, fruits, vegetables, etc.): approximately $50 per month

Your Budgerigars needs a varied and healthy diet. There's a massive selection of high quality seed diets, complete food and pelleted foods to choose from both online and in your local pet stores, not to mention some treats you might want to buy especially when they're doing tricks! The cost will depend on the brand as well as the nutritional value of the food.

Feeding a variety of these foods, alongside fruits and vegetables is the key to a healthy parrot.

Cleaning Supplies: at least $10 per month

You don't need brand new cleaning supplies every month, but of course, you will run out of bird shampoo and soap eventually. Just include it in your budget.

Veterinary Care: starts at $150 - $1,000 or more

Budgerigars rarely get sick compared to other types of parrots, but it's important to keep them healthy by taking them to an avian vet for medical check-up every now and then. Avian vets are trained specifically to work with exotic birds whereas a general practicing vet may not be familiar with their needs and treatments especially if they are sick, not to mention the medicines needed.

If in case, this happens it's better and wiser to set aside a portion of your budget for any medical needs that will come up.

Additional Costs: at least $10 per month

In addition to all of these monthly costs you should plan for occasional extra costs like repairs to your Budgerigars cage, replacement toys, food supplements, medicines etc. You won't have to cover these costs every month but you should include it in your budget to be safe.

Here is the overview of your total monthly expenses for the needs of your pet Budgerigars.

Monthly Costs for Budgerigars	
Cost Type	Approximate Cost
Bird Food	$50 (£37.61)
Cleaning Supplies	$10 (£7.52)
Veterinary Care (optional)	$150 (£112.83)
Additional Costs	$10 (£7.52)
Total	$220 (£165.48)

*Please note that these amounts are computed at the starting price and converted at the current exchange rate which is $1 = £0.75

Costs may vary.

Chapter Four: Tips in Buying Budgerigars

If you are still interested in reading this chapter, that only means one thing: you have already decided to buy a Budgerigar. Good choice, they are really down-to-earth, friendly and fun birds, you'll surely enjoy being with them!

Here you will learn tips and tricks on how to select healthy Budgerigars, where to find the right breeder as well as the laws and permit you need to be aware of before buying.

Restrictions and Regulations in United States

If you are planning to acquire a Budgerigar as your pet, then you have to think beyond the cage. There are certain restrictions and regulations that you need to be aware of, because it will not only serve as protection for your bird but also for you. Here are some things you need to know regarding the acquirement of Budgerigars both in United States and in Great Britain.

a.) What is CITES?

CITES stands for Convention on International Trade in Endangered Species of Wild Fauna and Flora. It protects Budgerigars by regulating its import, export, and re-export through an international convention authorized through a licensing system.

It is also an international agreement, drafted by the International Union for Conservation of Nature (IUCN), which aims to ensure that the trade in specimens of wild animals and plants does not threaten their survival.

Different species are assigned in different appendix statuses such as Appendix I, II or III etc. These appendices indicate the level of threat to the current population of the bird with consideration to their likely ability to rebound in the wild with legal trade.

One of the advantages of the budgie parakeet is that it is NOT listed in CITES appendices, which simply means that **it does not require CITES permits.** Yes, you can travel with your budgie as much as you want without any restrictions, provided that you'll take care of them and not lose them.

Permits in Great Britain and Australia

In Great Britain and Australia you may need a permit for you to be able to import, export, or travel with your Budgerigars. This permit is called an **Animal Movement License**.

Aside from the CITES permit, sometimes a Pet Bird Import License and a veterinary health certificate are required before bringing your bird in Great Britain, the purpose of this is to prevent the spread of diseases if the bird is a carrier.

You can apply for a Pet Bird Import License through this link: <http://AHITchelmsford@animalhealth.gsi.gov.uk.>

Like in the United States being aware of the regulations and getting a license is an important thing you need to consider before you acquire, import or export a bird. This does not only protect the animals but it can also avoid confiscation of your pet.

Practical Tips in Buying Budgerigars

Now that you are already aware and have prior knowledge about the legal aspects of owning a Budgerigar, the next step is purchasing one through a local pet store or a legitimate breeder.

Here are some recommendations for finding a reputable Budgerigar parrot breeders in United States and in Great Britain.

How to Find a Budgerigar Breeder

The first thing you need to do is to look for a legit avian breeder or pet store in your area that specializes in Budgerigars.

You can also find great avian breeders online but you have to take into consideration the validity of the breeder. It is highly recommended that you see your new bird in person before buying anything on the internet. You can find several recommended list of Budgerigar local breeder websites later in this book.

If possible, spend as much time as you can with your prospective new Budgerigars before buying it. Interact with the bird and see how it is with you.

Continue the diet of the bird as advised by the store owner or breeder to maintain its eating habits. Look for any health problems or issues as well.

Finally, only purchase a Budgerigar that is banded. Banding means the bird have a small metal band on one of its legs placed at birth by the breeder which is inscribed with the bird's clutch number, date of birth and the breeder number.

Leg bands are indicators that the purchaser and the bird itself are in the country legally and have not been smuggled.

Local Budgerigars Breeders in the United States

Here are the lists of available Budgerigar breeders in the United States. Availability and costs of these Budgerigars may vary over time, please check the links provided for any updates.

Birdman's Baby Parrots

5668 N Lincoln Ave Chicago, Illinois

Website: www.birdmansparrots.com

Tel. No.: 773-317-3785

AJ'S Feathered Friends

804 N. La Fox Street. South Elgin, IL 60177

Website: www.ajspetshop.com

Tel. No.: 847-695-5624

Something Cheeky

Clayton, North Carolina 27520

Website: www.somethingcheeky.com

Tel. No.: 1-919-585-2241

In A Pickle Parrots

7924 Broadview Road, Broadview Heights, Ohio 44147

Website: www.inapickleparrots.com

Tel. No.: 440-627-6477

Email: Inapickleaviary@aol.com

World of Birds

15 Perry Street, Chester, New Jersey 07930

Website: www.worldofbirds.com

Tel. No.: 908-879-2291

Email: worldofbirds@optonline.net

Morning Glory Birds

West Hempstead, New York 11552

Website: www.facebook.com/glory.birds.7

Tel. No.: 516-972-3860

Featherheads

Port charlotte, Florida 33948

Website:http://www.birdbreeders.com/breeder/13627/feathe
rheads-florida-port-charlotte-FL

Tel. No.: 813-679-4961

Ginos Exiotic Birds

Blue Jay, CA 92317

Website: http://www.birdbreeders.com/bird

Tel. No.: 176-095-604-66

Email: Gmorrialle@gmail.com

Fancy Feathers

31 Roseland Avenue, Caldwell, New Jersey

Website: www.fancyfeathersaviary.com

Tel. No.: 973-403-2900

E-mail: ddargenio@gmail.com

The Bird Lady

17044 I-20, Lindale, Texas 75771

Website: http://www.birdbreeders.com/breeder/7816/the-bird-lady-east-of-dallas-off-of-i-20-TX/reviews

Tel. No.: 956-309-0750

E-mail: debinmcallen@att.net

SpringOak

Dripping Springs, Texas 78620

Website:http://www.birdbreeders.com/breeder/5561/springoak-dripping-springs-TX

Tel. No.: 512-630-1626

Email: sherylcoffman1@gmail.com

The Parrots Nest Of Maryland

4508 G Lower Beckleysville Road, Hampstead, Mary Land

Website: http://www.birdbreeders.com/bird/

Tel. No.: 410-374-1636

Email: livesaybrian@aol.com

Linville's Aviary

Miami, Florida 33174

Website:http://www.birdbreeders.com/breeder/2920/linvilles
-aviary-miami-FL

Tel. No.: 305-968-1536

E-mail: cerbyu@aol.com

Avian Events, LLC

Conyers, GA 30094

Website: www. avianevents.com

Tel. No.: 770-500-2882

Email: tom@avianevents.com

The Parrots Nest Of Maryland

4508 G Lower Beckleysville Road, Hampstead, Mary Land

Website: http://www.birdbreeders.com/bird/

Tel. No.: 410-374-1636

Email: livesaybrian@aol.com

Green Parrot Superstore

8165 S. State Rd, Goodrich, Michigan

Website: www.greenparrotsuperstore.com

Tel. No.: 810-636-9120

Email: greenparrotsuperstore@gmail.com

Thea's Parrot Place

Fallbrook, California 92028

Website: www.theasparrotplace.com

Tel. No.: 760-842-3436

Email: theasparrotplace@att.net

Tail Feathers

Durand, Illinois 61024

Website: http://www.birdbreeders.com/breeder/38015/tail-feathers-durand-IL

Tel. No.: 815-248-4035

Email: tgsmall49@live.com

Birds By Joe LLC

1309 Bound Brook Road, Middlesex, NJ 08846

Website: www.birdsbyjoe.com

Tel. No.: 732-764-2473

Email: service@birdsbyjoe.com

Above the Rainbow Aviary

Gallipolis Ferry, West Virginia 25515

Website:http://www.birdbreeders.com/breeder/10444/above-the-rainbow-aviary-gallipolis-ferry-WV

Tel. No.: 304-812-4340

Email: abovetherainbowaviary@comcast.net

Tweety Bird Aviary

263 Hobbs Island Road, Huntsville, AL 35803

Website: www.tweetybirdaviary.com

Tel. No.: 256-656-2019

E-mail: LBroach487@Gmail.com

Whidbey Birds

P.O. Box 1682 Coupeville, Washington 98239

Website: www.whidbeybirds.com

Tel. No.: 360-929-2869

E-mail: whidbeybirds@msn.com

Birds Exotic

1060 S. Chester Ave. Delran, NJ 08075

Website: www.thebirdstore.com

Tel. No.: 856-764-2473

E-mail: thebirdstore@yahoo.com

Lone Palm Aviary

Loxahatchee, Florida 33470

Website: www.lpbirds.com

Tel. No.: 570-730-1366

Email: jessica@lpbirds.com

The Finch Farm Co.

Miami, Florida 33101

Website: www.thefinchfarm.com

Tel. No.: 877-527-5656

E-mail: jenna.thefinchfarm@gmail.com

Ara Aviaries California

Agoura Hills Los Angeles, California

Website: www.aracaris.com

Tel. No.: 805-338-3549

Email: billysaylors6@gmail.com

Ana's Parrots

East Stroudsburg, PA 18301

Website: https://www.facebook.com/PoconoAna

Tel. No.: 646-496-5005

E-mail: poconoana@yahoo.com

Parrotsrok

Skiatook, Oklahoma 74070

Website: http://parrotsrok.com/Home%20Page.html

Tel. No.: 918-289-8787

E-mail: mandmok@sbcglobal.net

The Parrot's Cove

New Iberia, Los Angeles 70560

Website: theparrotcove.com

Tel. No.: 337-519-3943

E-mail: theparrotscove@theparrotcove.com

5 Oaks Aviary

Oklahoma City, Oklahoma 73150

Website: www.fiveoaksaviary.com

Tel. No.: 405-209-4312

E-mail: fiveoaksaviary@msn.com

Debbie's Birdhouse

32 East Harrison Street Tunkhannock, Pennsylvania 18657

Website: www.debbiesbirdhouse.com

Tel. No.: 570-240-7268

E-mail: Debbie57@ptd.net

Pet Paradise

35535 Euclid Avenue, Willoughby, Ohio

Website: www.petparadiseohio.com

Tel. No.: 440-942-9016

E-mail:info@petparadiseohio.com

The Bird Hut

Nashville, Tennessee 37221

Website: www.the-bird-hut.com

Tel. No.: 615-739-0631

E-mail: midtnecho@yahoo.com

Delorce's Bird Barn

Charleston, South Carolina 29429

Website: www.delorcesbirdbarn.com

Tel. No.: 8432161553 or 8438198618

Email: brendabrinson1234@gmail.com

Toucan Jungle

Vista, CA 92084

Website: www.ToucanJungle.com

Tel. No.: 760-672-0127

Email: Chris@Toucanjungle.com

Bill and Kennys family birds

135 Terry Road Hartford, Connecticut 06105

Website: http://www.birdbreeders.com/breeder/26465/bill-and-kennys-family-birds-hartford-CT

Tel. No.: 203 441-0366

Email:billsbirdsnbeaks@gmail.com

Kedzie Parrot Place

East Lansing, Michigan 48823

Website: www.kedzieparrotplace.com

Tel. No.: 517-204-3878

Email: kedzieparrotplace@hotmail.com

Cindy's Parrot Place

Chesapeake, Virginia 23321

Website: http://www.cindysparrotplace.com

Tel. No.: 1-844-572-7768

Email: info@cindysparrotplace.com

Local Budgerigars Breeders in Great Britain

Here are the website links and contact details of local Budgerigars breeders in Great Britain:

UK Breeder Websites

Hand Reared Parrots

<http://www.handrearedparrots.co.uk/>

Bird Trader

<http://www.birdtrader.co.uk/>

PreLoved

<http://www.preloved.co.uk/>

Selecting a Healthy Budgerigar

Budgerigars on average can live for up to 15 - 20 years and more! These birds are long time companions, and its longevity highly depends on how your chosen breeders took care of them especially when they were young.

This section will give you simple tips on how you can spot a healthy Budgerigar that you can keep for life!

a.) Signs of a Healthy Budgerigar

Look out for these signs so that you know if your prospect bird is healthy:

- The bird should be active, alert, and sociable
- It should eat and drink throughout the day
- It should have dry nostrils and bright, dry eyes
- The beak, legs, and feet should have normal appearance
- It should have a dry and clean vent
- Its feathers should be smooth and well-groomed

Chapter Five: Maintenance for Budgerigars

Assuming that you have already bought a Budgerigar as your pet, the responsibility that comes with it is the most crucial part of the process. You as the owner, have to provide for its basic needs so that it will be healthy and happy. In this chapter you will learn the different requirements needed for your bird such as its cage, accessories and food necessary for the maintenance of your Budgerigars.

Habitat and Environment

Budgerigars have adapted well to human-modified habitats, such as parks and gardens in villages and towns. Like other kinds of birds, Budgerigars should be kept in a bird-safe environment. As the owner you need to have knowledge of its habitat requirements and environmental conditions to ensure that your bird is healthy. You will find tons of information in this section regarding the maintenance your pet needs in order to keep them happy.

a.) Ideal Cage Size for Budgerigars

Budgerigars, like other birds, loves lots of space when it is inside its cage. A general guideline that you can follow when it comes to bird cages is that, the parrot should not have restricted movements and should be able to flap its wings without touching the sides of the cage.

It is also advisable to buy a durable cage preferably with locks to prevent them from escaping because they are naturally curious and quite naughty at times.

The cage should ideally provide room for both horizontal exercise and vertical climbing. A minimum of 24"x16"x16" (70x40x40cm) with no more than half an inch (1.3 cm) bar spacing is the recommended cage size for Budgerigars.

It is also advisable that the cage material uses non-toxic paint or else it can cause your pet to be poisoned by metal. It shouldn't also be made out of brass either because it contains zinc which could kill your parrot as well.

Ideally the cage should also have at least three doors. One as the main entrance and the other two should be used for food and water.

Your bird will be spending most of their lives inside the cage that's why it needs to be large so that it can also accommodate lots of toys and perches.

b.) Cage Maintenance

Your parrot's cage could affect the health of your pet so it's very important that you check it daily for any dirt, like its feces and spoiled food left in perches and cups to prevent health problems.

You should also change the cage paper every other day as well as check the metal parts & bars of your bird's cage periodically for chipped paint and rust, because your bird will most likely chew or swallow the flaked pieces.

You should be able to clean the cage thoroughly at least once every month. You could use a mild dishwashing liquid or bleach with warm water for about a minute. Then rinse all soap and bleach thoroughly with water before letting your bird inside the cage.

c.) Location of the Cage

Finding the perfect cage is just as important as knowing where to place it. As established earlier, Budgerigars are most of the time too talkative and noisy, that's why you should also take that into consideration when finding a good location for your bird.

Put them in a place where they'll get to interact with people, and won't be too much of a disturbance at the same time – if in case they talk non-stop, and they will!

Put the cage at an eye level to create a sense of confidence in your bird and place the cage in a higher location so that they would feel secure just like in the wild.

Avoid placing the cage near dangerous fumes or drafts, this might kill them. Do not also place it directly in a window because the sun can cause your parrot to become ill due to too much heat. If it helps you can at least find a shade or cover for the cage, so that your bird may get just the right amount of heat during the day and feel comfortable during night time.

Finding the right location of the cage could lessen stressful situations for your bird so that they can enjoy their life with their new owner.

d.) Recommended Supplies

Now that your cage is all set and you already have an idea on where to properly place it, you need to provide supplies to meet its needs. Here are the recommended supplies that your Budgerigars needs:

Perches

The main purpose of perches is to exercise your bird's feet; it could also prevent sores and foot related health issues in the future. In the wild, birds like Budgerigars, are used to transferring from one tree to another but in captivity of course they can't do that, so a great alternative is to buy them perches, preferably made out of fresh fruit tree branches. The minimum area for the perch is about ¾" - 1" (2 - 2.5 cm) in diameter.

You can buy different types of perches such as wood dowel, natural branch type, a therapeutic perch or a cement perch as well as Eucalyptus branches; just make sure that it is not poisonous.

Budgerigars also love to gnaw perches, and because of that you may have to replace it regularly. There are lots of perches you could choose from especially from online stores. These perches could also be used as ropes and swings for your pet. Do not put the perch above the bird's bowl or dishes otherwise the food and water will be contaminated.

Toys

Budgerigars are very playful and active and like any other birds, they will chew anything, you may find yourself regularly buying and replacing new toys to keep them happy. It is recommended that you purchase toys that are easy to be destroyed, it'll be very interactive for your Budgerigars to prevent boredom. However, if you're in a tight budget, you can also buy toys that are durable so that it could last longer. There are a lot of toys online and in pet stores that you can buy for your Budgerigar.

It is not advisable to put all of the toys inside your bird's cage because it will become dirty and overcrowded. Rotate the toys at least once a week.

Dishes

Buy at least 3 sturdy dishes; one for fresh water, one for pellet or seed mix and one for fresh foods. Avoid buying plastic dishes because your Budgerigars will most likely break it and it could also be harmful to its health. Place it away from the perches so that it would not be contaminated with bird droppings.

Formulated Diet

Some Budgerigars owners feed their birds only with seeds, while some only provides a pellet diet; this however could limit the nutrients your pet is receiving.

Experts suggest that parrots should be given a variety of food for a balanced nutrition or what they call a formulated diet.

Budgerigars are a very energetic and lively parrot that's why a good combination of formulated diet (seeds, fruits and vegetables) as well as a good amount of protein and other nutrients plus clean water is essential to keep their bodies healthy and active.

You will need a good supply of packaged pellet diet, to be mixed with seed. Then you can slowly add fresh foods and protein. Formulated bird food may already contain vitamins so it's not recommended that you give another one separately unless prescribed by your vet. Conversion takes about a week or so depending on your bird and how well you feed them.

Treats

Budgerigars can also be taught to perform different kinds of tricks and should undergo "bird training", but of course, it always comes with a price! You can give your pet different types of treats such as fruits, seed and spray as well as Do-It-Yourself (DIY) treats like pretzels, popcorn or something healthy that your bird can munch on. Later in this book, you will be provided with a list of recommended treats as well as treats you should avoid.

e.) Bird Bath for Budgerigars

Budgerigars need a regular bath ideally in the morning, to maintain a good skin condition. Here are some things you need to know on how to maintain your bird's hygiene and keep a healthy life.

Provide a misting bottle or a birdbath. All birds should be gently misted with a water bottle at room temperature. The spray should be sprayed up over the bird much like a shower rain, never spray the bird directly in its face.

It's important that you keep an eye in your bird while it is bathing. Bathe your Budgerigar with clean water. Distilled water is sometimes required. Speak to your veterinarian on the best choice of water for your bird. During its misting and bathing procedures, make sure there are no drafts because it can cause respiratory issues. It may chill your bird when he is wet. Use towels and blankets, but be careful because it can catch the bird's nails and beaks in their threads.

To ensure that the oils from their skin glands, disease organisms or items such as lotions and hand creams do not transfer to your bird's feathers, wash your hands with soap and water thoroughly before handling your Budgerigar.

Your bird may be ill if it seems to stop grooming and becomes dirty. Once you see this signs, contact your avian veterinarian immediately.

f.) Lighting and Environmental Temperature

The average room temperature for your Budgerigars should be anywhere between 65-75°F (18 - 24°C). Also avoid drafty areas that will get direct heat from sun for any portion of the day.

Parrots also have tetra-chromic vision (4 color light vision including ultraviolet), that's why a full color light bulb must be present in the cage area. The incandescent or monochromatic light bulbs usually found in households are not a good choice for your Budgerigars.

Cover the cage during nighttime or at least provide a shade to block out any excess light and also creates a more secure sleeping place. Be careful when using fabrics as cover because your bird might rip it with its claws or beak and could likely eat it.

Never ever place the cage in the kitchen or somewhere near cooking fumes because bird's can be very sensitive, that even a small amount of smoke can be fatal.

Diet and Feeding

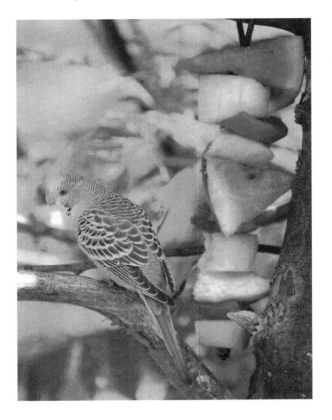

In the wild, Budgerigars primarily eat palm nuts, seeds and fruits. Since these birds are very active, they will need nutrients that are rich in calories, protein and fats among others.

Fortunately, today's supplements have opened new and healthy options for pet owners. In this section you will be guided on how to properly feed your parrot and learn the feeding amount and nutritional requirements they need.

a.) Nutritional Needs of Budgerigars

Feeding your Budgerigars is not that complicated. However, its level of activity should be taken into consideration to meet its nutritional diet. They're not choosy eaters but like what was mentioned earlier, it is highly recommended that parrots should be given a variety of food for a balanced nutrition.

As much as possible avoid only giving the same type of food such as a pellet diet or seed diet only; it can result in nutrient deficiency and may lead to diseases due to its limited nutrients, which could also shorten the life expectancy of your parrot.

This section outlines the foods your pet will appreciate in order to meet the majority of its dietary needs.

b.) Types of Food

Seeds and Pellet

Seeds are a big part of any bird's diet; they eat seeds naturally in the wild and it is also a good source of Carbohydrates. However, seeds alone can cause complications because it is naturally fatty. Although some Budgerigars need fatty acids for their skin development, it still should be moderated. It is not advisable that you mixed seeds with pellets and feed it off right away, although a lot of people do recommend that; for best results offer seeds first for a few days, then slowly incorporate pellets into the diet until your Budgerigar gets well adjusted.

The key is to give it in moderation. Feed them at least 1/8 - 1/4 cup of fortified parrot mix or diet, the amount may vary depending on how much your Budgerigar can consume.

Fresh Vegetables

Vegetables contain Phytonutrients that enhance the body's immune system which prevents illnesses. Veggies are also a rich source of natural fiber for the body. However, keep in mind that you should feed them with vegetables in moderation to prevent diarrhea and make sure they are properly washed before feeding it to your bird.

Below is the list of highly recommended vegetables for Budgerigars:

- Artichoke
- Asparagus
- Beets and greens
- Broccoli and greens
- Cabbage
- Carrots
- Cauliflower and greens
- Celery
- Chard

- Chickweed
- Chicory
- Chinese Cabbage
- Cucumber
- Dandelion Greens
- Edamame
- Eggplant
- Fennel and leaves, stems, seeds
- Kale
- Leeks
- Lettuce (darker is better)
- Mustard Greens
- Okra
- Peas/Snap Peas/String Beans/Snow Peas
- Peppers (all types)
- Radicchio
- Radish and greens
- Spinach
- Sweet Potato/Yam (cooked/parboiled)
- Squash (all types)
- Tomatoes (offer in moderation)
- Turnips and turnip greens
- Watercress
- Wheat Grass
- Yams

Fruits

Fruits are healthy and sweet; they also provide natural sources of sugars for the parrots. It is recommended that you only offer bite-sized fruits and do remove the pits or seeds of the fruits to prevent your Budgerigars from choking.

Below are list of fruits that are highly recommended by veterinarians for your Budgerigars:

- Apples (no seed)
- Apricots (no seed)
- Banana
- Blackberries
- Blueberries
- Cherries (no seed)
- Coconut (feed sparingly due to fat content)
- Cranberries
- Custard Apple
- Dragon Fruit
- Figs
- Guava
- Grapefruit
- Grapes
- Kiwi Fruit
- Lemon
- Lime
- Longan
- Lychee

phenylalanine and valine that some Budgerigars are not able to produce or sustain in its body. Fortunately, the sources of these essential amino acids are available in today's bird diet products.

Here is the list of recommended protein for your pet Budgerigars to feed on:

- Beans (cook small amounts as needed)
- Chicken (cooked, preferably shredded not fried)
- Eggs (cooked/hard boiled)
- Nuts (all types)
- Peanuts
- Seeds (birdseeds provide protein)
- Sprouts
- Turkey (cooked, preferably shredded)
- Meal Worms (feed it occasionally)

Calcium

Calcium's primary role is to make bones grow stronger and it also allows calcification of eggshells in birds. In captivity, you can provide calcium in the form of a cuttlebone or calcium treat that is attached inside your bird cage. You can also offer a powdered supplement such as packaged oyster shell which can be added directly to your pet's food. Follow the instructions on the supplement package. Calcium is also vital for muscle contraction, blood clotting and heart functions.

It is optional that your Budgerigars be exposed to UVB light for at least 3-4 hours a day; this may help for its optimal physiologic use of the calcium you are giving to your bird.

Water

Hydration is just as important for birds as it is for human beings especially during hot weather conditions to avoid dehydration; Budgerigars may drink 10 times its normal water intake during summer. They should be given access to clean, fresh and cool water. Do not use tap water because can cause the bird to be ill, as well as distilled water, instead use unflavored bottled drinking water or bottled natural spring water. If in case, tap water is used, treat it with a de-chlorinating treatment. Inability to provide fresh water to pet birds can cause upset stomach with unbearable stomachache.

Water is vital to maintain cells, digestion, feathers, and metabolism.

All water given to birds for drinking, as well as water used for misting, soaking or bathing must be 100% free of chlorine and heavy metals.

Treats

As mentioned earlier, you could give your parrots a reward every time they do something right like performing tricks or simply learning how to speak. You can feed them with different types of nuts such as almonds, macadamias, and walnuts. You can also give easy to digest and bite-sized fruits or Do-It-Yourself treats every now and then.

Some examples of DIY treats are carrot muffins (minus the sugar), popcorn, corn, unsalted pretzel sticks with fruits and brown rice with berries. They will surely love something appetizing to eat and this is also a positive reinforcement for the bird especially during training them.

c.) Toxic Foods to Avoid

Some foods are specifically toxic for your Budgerigars or any type of birds in general. Make sure that your bird never gets to eat one of the toxic items below and ensure that an avian veterinary checks your bird every now and then. These harmful foods is as important as selecting the right supplements and food items for your bird.

The following list of foods is highly toxic for your Budgerigars:

- Onions
- Alcohol
- Mushrooms
- Tomato Leaves
- Caffeine

- Dried Beans
- Parsley
- Chocolate (highly allergic)
- Avocados
- Junk Food
- Apple and Cherry Seeds
- Lettuce
- Milk and Dairy Products
- French fries,
- Marbled meat
- Peanut Butter
- Butter

Handling and Training Budgerigars

There would be instances that your pet will be out of its cage, especially for Budgerigars. These birds are very active and naturally playful and outgoing. However, it's also important to keep in mind on how to properly handle and train your Budgerigars so that it will not cause harm to itself and to people as well.

In this section, you'll learn some guidelines on how to confidently handle your parrot as well as some tips on trimming its nails, wings and beaks to maximize its balance, abilities and flying potential.

a.) Tips for Taming Your Budgerigars

Taming your Budgerigar is the first thing to do before teaching them some cool tricks.

The flipside of owning a budgie is that they have quite a reputation for being a bit mischievous, in some cases they even tend to bite when feel threatened. The key is to figure out the level of your bird's comfort zone and remove it so that you could have a great bonding experience together. Here are some tips on how to do tame your budgie:

- Start by slowly touching your parrot in its beak. Carefully move your hand closer and closer towards its beak. If the parrot reacts or moves away, stop for a while.
- Wait for it to calm down, then take your hand away and give a treat.
- Practices repeating this procedure until you are able to fully touch its beak. Your Budgerigars will eventually tolerate you in touching its beak and once you do, you can also scratch their beak. Just be extra careful when doing it, their beaks are sharp and really strong, but you have to conquer your fear if you want to get along with them!

b.) Tips for Training Your Budgerigars

Now that you and your budgie quite get along already, strengthen your relationship by training them some basic lessons.

Training a Budgerigar is not that hard to do, in fact it can be a fun and rewarding bonding experience for you and your feathered friend! There are lots of pet owners out there who have properly trained and raised a well-behaved Budgerigar. They are clever creatures by nature, that is why they can absorb information very quickly and easily as long as you do it right.

Trust is the most important key in training your parrot. The first thing you need to do is to be able to establish a solid connection and rapport between you and your pet.

This section will provide some guidelines you can follow in getting your bird well behaved and disciplined. Are you ready? Read on!

Stepping Up is a basic skill your parrot should learn, to find out how to do this follow the tips below:

- A good way to pacify your bird into your hands without being forceful is to try and make your parakeet step up onto a handheld perch.
- Slowly and progressively begin training it to step up on your hand. If you are afraid of being bitten then

wear gloves, but you may want to get rid of it eventually because it might still encourage them to bite you because they can chew the leather.

- Hold your hand in a short distance away from your parrot so that when it tries to step into the target stick, it will have no choice but to step into your hand.
- Keep practicing until your parrot won't need your stick anymore. It will get accustomed and comfortable whenever you command it to step up in your finger

Grooming Your Budgerigars

a.) Trimming Your Budgerigar's Nails

Like many parrots, Budgerigar have a sharp, needle-like nails because they do a lot of climbing in the wild, and they also use these nails to dig into wood to keep them secure.

Unclipped nails can dig into the skin, leaving scratches or painful wounds to a person, only clipped to a point that the bird can perch securely and does not bother you when the bird is perched on your hand. Many people have their Budgerigar's nails clipped to the point that it becomes dull and the bird can no longer grip a perch firmly.

This can result to becoming more clumsy and nervous because it cannot move without slipping. This nervousness can develop into fear biting and panic attacks.

Another tip is only use a styptic powder on your bird's nails, not the skin!

b.) Trimming Your Budgerigar's Beaks

Although, Budgerigars can pretty much maintain its beak's from deformity on its own, it's still important that you keep them in good condition. They are very fond of chewing and pecking everything they can get into. That's why it may eventually become dull which could also lead to deformation if not properly cared for.

Consult a qualified veterinarian to show you the proper way in trimming your pet's beaks. You can also check out several grooming items such as lava and mineral blocks that are available in your local pet store, to keep their beaks in great shape.

c.) Clipping a Budgerigar's Wings

Birds are design to fly, young Budgerigars can be fairly clumsy and flying gives them confidence as well as agility, stamina, and muscle tone.

Before clipping their wings, make sure that your Budgerigars are flying, maneuvering and landing well already. If they do not learn how to properly land by lifting their wings and flaring their tail, then when they are clipped, they could injure themselves and could also break their beak or keel bone.

Consult a qualified veterinarian to show you the proper way in clipping a bird's wings. A certain amount of flight feathers will be removed while leaving the smaller balancing feathers inside the wing closer to the body uncut.

Chapter Six: Breeding Budgerigars

If you decided to buy two Budgerigars, for instance a male and female and keep them together, you should definitely prepare for the possibility of breeding, unless it's the same gender, otherwise you're going to be caught off guard!

If you are interested in breeding your Budgerigars, this chapter will give you a wealth of information about the processes and phases of its breeding and you will also learn how to properly breed them on your own. This is not for everyone but if you want to have better understanding about how these birds procreate, then you should definitely not miss this part! On the contrary if you are interested in becoming a reputable breeder, then this is a must read chapter for you.

Basic Budgerigars Breeding Info

Before deciding if you truly want to become a breeder, you should at least have prior knowledge on their basic reproduction process and breeding. This section will inform you on how these creatures procreate.

a.) Sexual Dimorphism

Budgerigars are sexually dimorphic; males and females are visually identical. Female budgies are have white or light-blue, tan, or brown cere (head) while males commonly have blue or purplish-blue cere except for color mutated species. However, for the purpose of being accurate, it is best that your bird go through DNA analysis, which uses sample blood or feathers. Although, some breeders claim that they can distinguish if the bird is male or female because of its features, it is still indefinite unless it's DNA is tested.

DNA Sexing or Surgical Sexing can also provide additional information on its sexual maturity and capability to reproduce. It is inexpensive and convenient so if you like to know more about your bird's sexuality you should definitely give it a try. Some veterinarians might also try chromosomal analysis on your macaw to determine its gender.

b.) Mating and Reproduction

Budgerigars are typically monogamous when it comes to finding its mate. The breeding period for these birds usually occurs from June to September and once they start breeding, they'll continuously breed every year.

In terms of reproduction, Budgerigars reach their sexual maturity as early as 6 months old; females' clutch size ranges from 4 – 6 eggs with a maximum 7 - 10 eggs and incubation lasts for about 18 - 21 days.

The chicks become independent and leave the nest in when they reach approximately 50 - 60 days.

It is highly recommended that you provide an additional 20% increase on fatty seeds as well as their intake of vitamin supplements and proteins such as hard-boiled egg and shredded chicken during the breeding process.

It's also important to note that the incubation temperature should be kept between 37.2° - 37.3 °C (99.1°- 99.2°F) and humidity level should be at about 50 – 55% before the eggs are hatched.

The Budgerigar Breeding Process

In order to have a clear sketch of how Budgerigars reproduce, this section will show you the breeding process and the information you need to know, so that your pets can successfully procreate.

a.) Selecting Budgerigars for Breeding

For you to select a healthy, fertile and active parrot it is recommended that your parrot undergoes clinical examination by a veterinarian. This is essential to determine if your parrot is capable of reproduction or not and at the same time it can prevent diseases that could be transmitted to the coming flock.

b.) Setting up a Good Nesting Environment

Budgerigars in the wild usually nest in tree hollows or cliff openings; in captivity, you need to set up a nice environment to replicate that natural breeding and dwelling place so that they can successfully mate and create healthy clutches. The nest box size should ideally measure 12"x12"x12" (30 x 30 x 30 cm).

Keep in mind that the box should be three times the size of your Budgerigars. It is highly recommended that the nest box is wide so that your Budgerigars can have lots of space to move around and that it should ideally be made out of oak wood or metal.

The nest box should have a circular or round entrance hole that has an opening of about 3 inches (7.62 cm). Make sure that a strong wire is attached to the outside walls of the nest to prevent from escaping. To be able to help stabilize the eggs you can add about 2 inches of suitable nest box litter at the bottom of the box. Providing this may also be beneficial in absorbing the droppings from the chicks

c.) Nesting Materials

If you prefer to build your own nest box instead of buying one, you have to make sure that the materials you use are strong so that it will have a good foundation otherwise, your budgerigars could easily destroy it.

You should also put short pieces of wood or wood chips inside the box for your birds to chew; you can also give them bite-sized timber. Just make sure that it is large enough to not let the small chicks accidentally ingest it. This may help the breeders increase the percentage of fertile eggs and synchronize their breeding cycle as well.

d.) Brooding and Incubation

Budgerigars breed all year round but breeding season usually happens around spring time. Smaller species of

Budgerigars reach their sexual maturity as early as 6 months old; females' clutch size ranges from 4 – 6 eggs with a maximum 7 - 10 eggs and incubation lasts for about 18 - 21 days.

Generally, there is a 1 – 2 days interval for female Budgerigars after the first egg is laid. The chicks become independent and leave the nest in usually in 1 – 2 months or approximately 50 – 60 days.

e.) Hatching

On average, the eggs hatch in about 24 – 48 hours after the incubation period for Budgerigars and it takes about 1 – 2 months before the young Budgerigars leave the nest. Consult your vet on the suitable type of diet and vitamins or supplements needed for your baby Budgerigars.

Hybridization of Budgerigars

Hybrids are the offspring of parents of different species, subspecies or races. Cross-breeding is quite common especially within genera. Hybrids are a wonderful mixture of colors and they have interracial qualities, which makes it way more expensive than regular budgies, so it's favorable for pet traders.

Generally, there are three generations of hybrid in parrots; the first-generation hybrid is a crossing of two natural occurring species. The second-generation hybrid is a natural Budgerigars specie combined with a first-generation hybrid, while the third-generation hybrid is the product of crossing hybrid Budgerigars (either first or second generation).

Some bird enthusiasts and experts are against the practice of hybridization because it affects the naturally occurring bird population. If you would like to breed a hybrid Budgerigars, it is best to consult with your avian veterinarian first to check if your parrot has the capability to reproduce and to also avoid diseases.

a.) List of Hybrid Budgerigar Breeders in United States

Below are the lists of hybrid Budgerigars breeders in United States, please be reminded that these Budgerigars may be more expensive than their usual price. The rarer the species, the more expensive it could be. The availability and prices of these birds may also vary.

Green Parrot Superstore

8165 S. State Rd, Goodrich, Michigan

Website: www.greenparrotsuperstore.com

Tel. No.: 810-636-9120

Email: greenparrotsuperstore@gmail.com

Thea's Parrot Place

Fallbrook, California 92028

Website: www.theasparrotplace.com

Tel. No.: 760-842-3436

Email: theasparrotplace@att.net

Tail Feathers

Durand, Illinois 61024

Website: http://www.birdbreeders.com/breeder/38015/tail-feathers-durand-IL

Tel. No.: 815-248-4035

Email: tgsmall49@live.com

Birds By Joe LLC

1309 Bound Brook Road, Middlesex, NJ 08846

Website: www.birdsbyjoe.com

Tel. No.: 732-764-2473

Email: service@birdsbyjoe.com

Above the Rainbow Aviary

Gallipolis Ferry, West Virginia 25515

Website:http://www.birdbreeders.com/breeder/10444/above-the-rainbow-aviary-gallipolis-ferry-WV

Tel. No.: 304-812-4340

Email: abovetherainbowaviary@comcast.net

Tweety Bird Aviary

263 Hobbs Island Road, Huntsville, AL 35803

Website: www.tweetybirdaviary.com

Tel. No.: 256-656-2019

E-mail: LBroach487@Gmail.com

Whidbey Birds

P.O. Box 1682 Coupeville, Washington 98239

Website: www.whidbeybirds.com

Tel. No.: 360-929-2869

E-mail: whidbeybirds@msn.com

Birds Exotic

1060 S. Chester Ave. Delran, NJ 08075

Website: www.thebirdstore.com

Tel. No.: 856-764-2473

E-mail: thebirdstore@yahoo.com

Birdmans Baby Parrots

5668 N Lincoln Ave Chicago, Illinois

Website: www.birdmansparrots.com

Tel. No.: 773-317-3785

AJ'S Feathered Friends

804 N. La Fox Street. South Elgin, IL 60177

Website: www.ajspetshop.com

Tel. No.: 847-695-5624

Something Cheeky

Clayton, North Carolina 27520

Website: www.somethingcheeky.com

Tel. No.: 1-919-585-2241

In A Pickle Parrots

7924 Broadview Road, Broadview Heights, Ohio 44147

Website: www.inapickleparrots.com

Tel. No.: 440-627-6477

Email: Inapickleaviary@aol.com

World of Birds

15 Perry Street, Chester, New Jersey 07930

Website: www.worldofbirds.com

Tel. No.: 908-879-2291

Email: worldofbirds@optonline.net

Morning Glory Birds

West Hempstead, New York 11552

Website: www.facebook.com/glory.birds.7

Tel. No.: 516-972-3860

Featherheads

Port charlotte, Florida 33948

Website:http://www.birdbreeders.com/breeder/13627/feathe
rheads-florida-port-charlotte-FL

Tel. No.: 813-679-4961

Ginos Exiotic Birds

Blue Jay, CA 92317

Website: http://www.birdbreeders.com/bird

Tel. No.: 176-095-604-66

Email: Gmorrialle@gmail.com

Fancy Feathers

31 Roseland Avenue, Caldwell, New Jersey

Website: www.fancyfeathersaviary.com

Tel. No.: 973-403-2900

E-mail: ddargenio@gmail.com

The Bird Lady

17044 I-20, Lindale, Texas 75771

Website: http://www.birdbreeders.com/breeder/7816/the-
bird-lady-east-of-dallas-off-of-i-20-TX/reviews

Tel. No.: 956-309-0750

E-mail: debinmcallen@att.net

SpringOak

Dripping Springs, Texas 78620

Website:http://www.birdbreeders.com/breeder/5561/springo
ak-dripping-springs-TX

Tel. No.: 512-630-1626

Email: sherylcoffman1@gmail.com

The Parrots Nest of Maryland

4508 G Lower Beckleysville Road, Hampstead, Mary Land

Website: http://www.birdbreeders.com/bird/

Tel. No.: 410-374-1636

Email: livesaybrian@aol.com

Linville's Aviary

Miami, Florida 33174

Website:http://www.birdbreeders.com/breeder/2920/linvilles
-aviary-miami-FL

Tel. No.: 305-968-1536

E-mail: cerbyu@aol.com

Avian Events, LLC

Conyers, GA 30094

Website: www. avianevents.com

Tel. No.: 770-500-2882

Email: tom@avianevents.com

Lone Palm Aviary

Loxahatchee, Florida 33470

Website: www.lpbirds.com

Tel. No.: 570-730-1366

Email: jessica@lpbirds.com

The Finch Farm Co.

Miami, Florida 33101

Website: www.thefinchfarm.com

Tel. No.: 877-527-5656

E-mail: jenna.thefinchfarm@gmail.com

Ara Aviaries California

Agoura Hills Los Angeles, California

Website: www.aracaris.com

Tel. No.: 805-338-3549

Email: billysaylors6@gmail.com

Ana's Parrots

East Stroudsburg, PA 18301

Website: https://www.facebook.com/PoconoAna

Tel. No.:   646-496-5005

E-mail: poconoana@yahoo.com

Parrotsrok

Skiatook, Oklahoma 74070

Website: http://parrotsrok.com/Home%20Page.html

Tel. No.: 918-289-8787

E-mail: mandmok@sbcglobal.net

The Parrot's Cove

New Iberia, Los Angeles 70560

Website: theparrotcove.com

Tel. No.: 337-519-3943

E-mail: theparrotscove@theparrotcove.com

5 Oaks Aviary

Oklahoma City, Oklahoma 73150

Website: www.fiveoaksaviary.com

Tel. No.: 405-209-4312

E-mail: fiveoaksaviary@msn.com

Debbie's Birdhouse

32 East Harrison Street Tunkhannock, Pennsylvania 18657

Website: www.debbiesbirdhouse.com

Tel. No.: 570-240-7268

E-mail: Debbie57@ptd.net

Cindy's Parrot Place

Chesapeake, Virginia 23321

Website: http://www.cindysparrotplace.com

Tel. No.: 1-844-572-7768

Email: info@cindysparrotplace.com

Linville's Aviary

Miami, Florida 33174

Website:http://www.birdbreeders.com/breeder/2920/linvilles
-aviary-miami-FL

Tel. No.: 305-968-1536

E-mail: cerbyu@aol.com

Delorce's Bird Barn

Charleston, South Carolina 29429

Website: www.delorcesbirdbarn.com

Tel. No.: 8432161553 or 8438198618

Email: brendabrinson1234@gmail.com

Toucan Jungle

Vista, CA 92084

Website: www.ToucanJungle.com

Tel. No.: 760-672-0127

Email: Chris@Toucanjungle.com

Bill and Kennys Family birds

135 Terry Road Hartford, Connecticut 06105

Website: http://www.birdbreeders.com/breeder/26465/bill-and-kennys-family-birds-hartford-CT

Tel. No.: 203 441-0366

Email:billsbirdsnbeaks@gmail.com

Kedzie Parrot Place

East Lansing, Michigan 48823

Website: www.kedzieparrotplace.com

Tel. No.: 517-204-3878

Email: kedzieparrotplace@hotmail.com

Pet Paradise

35535 Euclid Avenue, Willoughby, Ohio

Website: www.petparadiseohio.com

Tel. No.: 440-942-9016

E-mail:info@petparadiseohio.com

The Bird Hut

Nashville, Tennessee 37221

Website: www.the-bird-hut.com

Tel. No.: 615-739-0631

E-mail: midtnecho@yahoo.com

Chapter Seven: Keeping Budgerigars Healthy

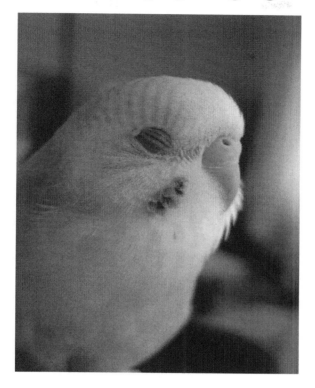

You as the owner should be aware of the potential threats and diseases that could harm the wellness of your Budgerigars. Just like human beings, you need to have knowledge on these diseases so that you can prevent it from happening in the first place. You will find tons of information on the most common problems that may affect your bird including its causes, signs and symptoms, remedies and prevention.

Common Health Problems

In this section, you will learn about the diseases that may affect and threaten your Budgerigar's wellness. Learning these diseases as well as its remedies is vital for you and your bird so that you could prevent it from happening or even help with its treatment in case they caught one.

Below are some of the most common health problems that occur specifically to Budgerigars parrots. You will learn some guidelines on how these diseases can be prevented and treated as well as its signs and symptoms.

Protozoal Infections

a.) Cause and Effect

Trichomonas and Giardia are common protozoal infections, these infections usually occurs during the breeding process of budgerigars. It spreads through breeding colonies of budgies.

b.) Signs and Symptoms

These protozoa usually target the intestines and digestive tract of the birds, which then causes diarrhea. If you think that your bird's feces is sticky rather than loose, it's a sign that your bird might be infected. As a precaution, you should bring him/her to a veterinarian for a lab report to prevent the infection

c.) Treatment and Remedy

The treatment for birds infected consists of several anti-parasitic medicines that are fortunately available to the vet, after which, your vet will suggest you to make your bird undergo lab tests to monitor and ensure that the medicine killed the virus.

<u>Avian Pox</u>

Avian pox is the single deadliest disease that acquired by Budgerigars. It is caused by an Avian Poxvirus infection and it causes real damage to Budgerigars and scarred it for life.

a.) Cause and Effect

The virus is usually transmitted through a direct contact with birds carrying the virus. Biting insects or any contaminated surfaces may spread the disease even further and may make the pain worse.

b.) Signs and Symptoms

The thickening of the eyes by mucous membranes is a sign that your Budgerigars is a carrier of the virus. It manifests through a wet form of the pox that affects, mouth, gullet, and upper and lower respiratory systems.

c.) Treatment and Remedy

Veterinarians typically recommend 10,000 units of Vitamin A which are given by injection. Antibiotics are also given to treat secondary infections and a Mercurochrome solution is given to treat their mucous-thickened eyes. Consult an avian veterinarian immediately.

E – Coli

Another common illness that affects Budgerigars is a bacteria called E-Coli. It is very rampant among psittacine birds.

a.) Cause and Effect

E-Coli is a gram-negative bacteria found in guts of birds that are considered abnormal; this bacteria is highly capable of causing diseases especially if it reaches into the bird's bloodstream, respiratory system, and reproductive system or if the carrier parrot is under a stressful situation.

b.) Signs and Symptoms

Coliform infections are the main cause of deaths in most Budgerigars, the E-Coli bacteria weakens the bird's digestive and respiratory system most of the time. A sudden loss appetite and difficulty in breathing may be a sign that your bird is suffering from this bacteria.

c.) Treatment and Remedy

Veterinarians usually have to determine first if these bacteria are the disease causing agents or merely a secondary infection through a culture testing before treating it with antibiotics or other necessary medicines.

Proventricular Dilation Disease

This disease is commonly known as Wasting Disease, it is rampant among Budgerigars species. It is an inflammatory wasting disease caused by a virus called Avian BornaVirus (ABV), which is mostly found in Psittacine species specially in Budgerigars. It primarily affects the Central Nervous System and multiple organs such as liver, kidneys, heart, brain, peripheral blood vessels, lungs and gastrointestinal tract.

a.) Cause and Effect

It is classified as a sporadic disease that has a very rare kind of attack to a bird's immune system. Unlike other virus which attacks the whole cell then move to another cell, ABV does not destroy the cells which leave the infected ones very little damage. Since the cells are not destroyed the immune system cannot detect it and thus the virus stays within the bird for an indefinite amount of time, which eventually weakens the immune system and results in continuous infections throughout the parrot's life.

c.) Diagnosis

Avian veterinarians have difficulties in detecting the virus because of other infections it can bring to the bird's health. The ABV does not show-up in the test results and there are other viruses similar to ABV which may also lead in the assumption that the bird is not a carrier even if it is.

d.) Signs and Symptoms

ABV is also an asymptomatic virus, which means that there are no signs that the bird might be infected or a carrier. However, sometimes you can notice it if your pet experienced instances of mild disorders such as moaning, feather-plucking or self-mutilation to severe illness such as head tremors, paralysis, seizures or other sudden sickness due to infected organs in the body.

e.) Treatment and Remedy

Veterinarians classified the severity of disease and level of impact to different stages such as low-to-moderate symptoms to severe and chronic stages.

Parrots in the early stages are given treatment to prevent the virus from spreading and eventually curing it. Although, this virus can be controlled and has a remedy, it's important that your bird always goes for checkup and undergo medical tests every now and then especially if it was diagnosed with the virus before.

Coacal Papilloma

It is caused by a virus infection similar to warts in other animals and it is transmitted through direct contact. These tiny tumors usually appear in the vent area of a Budgerigar where it can eventually block the fecal area of making it hard for the bird to defecate if it grows large enough.

a.) Treatment

The recommended treatment for this is a laser surgery. As a remedy veterinarians also advised owners to offer Jalapino peppers to prevent and control papilloma in birds. Consult your avian vet on the right amount of peppers to feed to your Budgerigars.

Psittacosis or Parrot Fever

It is a zoonotic infectious disease caused by an unknown organism whose natural hosts are birds such as Budgerigars.

a.) Cause and Effect

It is an airborne disease and it can also be spread via the bird's feces. This disease is highly contagious. Before acquiring a Budgerigar, it's important that your bird goes through a Psittacosis test because this type of infection can also potentially harm a human being.

b.) Signs and Symptoms

The worst thing about this disease is that it is asymptomatic, which means symptoms does not appear or cannot be detected easily, you will never know when it could happen and if the bird is a carrier. Nevertheless, watch out for these possible signs that your pet might be having Psittacosis:

- Difficulty in breathing (due to Respiratory infections with airsac)
- Sneezing
- Runny eyes
- Congestion
- Liver disease might occur (and can progress rapidly to death)

c.) Diagnosis of Psittacosis

As mentioned earlier, this type of disease is asymptomatic that sometimes even a psittacosis test could not detect the disease. Identifying organisms in the feces is done in most cases.

d.) Treatment and Remedy

This disease is treated with a tetracycline based antibiotic given for about 45 days to eliminate the carrier state, although some veterinarians believe that the antibiotic does not necessarily remove the carrier state.

Pacheco's Disease

This disease is caused by a herpes virus which attacks the liver and results in acute liver failure. It is very contagious and highly fatal to most birds.

a.) Diagnosis

Diagnosis is done via necropsy which detects microscopic evidences of the virus found in the liver.

b.) Treatment and Remedy

Unfortunately, there is no guaranteed antibiotic or remedy for this disease, the best you could do is to minimize the spread of the virus through intensive care and some antiviral medication.

Aspergillosis

It is a respiratory disease caused by the fungus called *Aspergillus,* which is found in warm and moist environments.

a.) Cause and Effect

The microscopic spores of Aspergillus are an airborne transmitted disease. The fungus does not cause the disease per se but if your bird does not have a healthy immune system it can cause illness.

It increases the chances of the spores being inhaled by your bird if the environment has poor ventilation and sanitation, dusty conditions, and in close confinements.

Other predisposing factors include poor nutrition, other medical conditions in the respiratory system and prolonged use of antibiotics or corticosteroids, which eventually weakens the immune system. Aspergillosis is more common in parrots than other pet birds.

b.) Signs and Symptoms

There are two kinds of Aspergillosis, it's either acute or chronic, both of which attacks the respiratory system.

Acute Aspergillosis signs and symptoms include:

- Severe difficulty in breathing
- Cyanosis (a bluish coloration of mucous membranes and/or skin)
- Decreased or loss of appetite
- Frequent drinking and urination

Chronic Aspergillosis symptoms include:

- White nodules appear through the respiratory tissue

- Large numbers of spores enter the bloodstream
- Infection in the kidneys, skin, muscle, gastrointestinal tract, liver, eyes, and brain

Other signs of Aspergillosis may include:

- Rapid breathing
- Exercise intolerance
- Change in syrinx (voice box); reluctance to talk
- Discharged and clogging of Nares
- Tremors
- Seizures or paralysis
- Green discoloration in the urates may be seen
- Enlarged liver
- Gout (painful, inflamed joints due to urate deposits)
- Depression and lethargy

c.) Diagnosis of Aspergillosis

Aspergillosis is generally difficult to detect until complete diagnosis. Do not compromise respiratory infections, consult the veterinarian immediately.
Here are some of the tests that your Budgerigars need to undergo through for diagnosis

- Radiographs (a complete blood count)
- Endoscopy (used to view lesions in the syrinx or

trachea)
- PCR testing for the presence of Aspergillus

d.) Treatment and Remedy

Always consult a veterinarian first to know the right remedy for your bird. There are reports that the antifungal drug Itraconazole may also be toxic to Budgerigars parrots than to other bird species. Another antifungal drug called Amphotericin B may be administered orally, topically, by injection, or nebulizing. Consult your vet for proper guidance. Surgery may also be performed to remove accessible lesions. Supportive care is often needed such as oxygen, supplemental heat, tube feeding, and treatment of underlying conditions.

e.) Prevention

Maintaining a good husbandry and diet can highly prevent outbreaks of Aspergillosis.

Below are some tips you can do to ensure that your bird is free from such a deadly disease:

- Keep your bird in a well-ventilated environment.
- Always clean the food and water dishes
- Thoroughly clean cages, toys, perches and other accessories at least once a month.
- Replace substrate (material lining the cage bottom)

regularly

- Offer a good nutrition, such as the right combination of fruits, vegetables and seeds

Psittacine Beak and Feather Disease (PBFD)

PBFD is a viral condition that is responsible for damage to the beak, feathers and nails as well as the immune system of infected birds. These are very common in parrots between 6 months and 3 years of age.

a.) Signs and symptoms

PBFD typically affects the feathers of infected birds as well as its beak and nails over time. Here are some signs and symptoms that your pet might have PBFD.

- Feathers are short, fragile, malformed, and prone to bleeding and breaking. Birds may first lose their the white, fine powder produced by specialized feathers to help maintain feather health when this happens more abnormal feathers will eventually develop.
- Beak has become glossy rather than the more typical matte appearance
- Nails and beak becomes brittle and malformed
- Significant loss of feathers (as the follicles become damaged)
- Loss of appetite (especially in young Budgerigars)
- Regurgitation or continuous vomiting

b.) Diagnosis

Veterinarians will likely perform a PCR test to confirm the diagnosis. This test uses advanced techniques to look for the virus' DNA.

Most of the time PCR only needs a blood sample, but your veterinarian may also need to take a swab from your bird's mouth and vent.

Other kinds of test may include:
- Complete blood count and a chemistry panel tests.
- DNA test for specifically for PBFD

c.) Treatment

The majority of clinically affected birds will die within a few months to a year because there are no antiviral drugs available to fight the virus. Your avian veterinarian can only help keep your bird comfortable because this condition is painful for the bird and it also allows secondary infections to take hold. Some birds may survive for a few months they will ultimately die from this disease.

d.) Prevention

The only thing breeders and pet owners can do to prevent this deadly virus is to take pro-active steps but since you can't help the birds mingle with other birds as they travel from wholesaler to retail pet distributors to your home the best solution is to have your bird examined by an avian veterinarian and allow diagnostic testing.

It is also wise to take your bird for a yearly exam to make sure it stays healthy. Yearly exams can catch small issues before they get worse.

Tracheal Mites

Tracheal Mites are quite common in birds because it can infiltrate the bird's entire respiratory tract and the severity of the infection can vary greatly. Birds with mild infections may not show any signs but severe infections may produce symptoms including trouble breathing, wheezing or clicking sounds, open-mouth breathing, and excessive salivation.

a.) Cause and Effect

This disease can be transmitted through close contact with an infected bird and through airborne particles. It can also be passed through contaminated food or drinking water.

b.) Diagnosis

It is quite difficult to diagnose if your Budgerigars has tracheal mites, veterinarians often recommend performing a tracheal swab to check under a microscope for further evaluation.

c.) Signs and Symptoms

Common signs include sneezing, wheezing or difficulty in breathing. Continuous bobbing of the tail while breathing is also a sign that you Budgerigar may have a respiratory problem. Tracheal mites also overlap with a number of other infections that has the same symptoms, so you need to make sure you have an accurate diagnosis.

d.) Treatment and Remedy

Medications are available to treat the disease, though dosage can be tricky and many birds die from tracheal mites. It is best to consult your veterinarian first before getting any treatment options available for tracheal mites.

Other common types of disorders and injuries in Budgerigars include:

- Constricted Toe
- Crop Burn
- Crop Punctures
- Dehydration
- Splay Leg
- Ruptured Air Sac
- Slipped Tendon
- Split Sternum
- Scissors Beak
- Sour and Slow Crop

- Sinusitis
- Salmonellosis
- Nasal Discharge
- Gout
- Beak and Feather Syndrome

Recommended Tests

Here are the recommended tests your Budgerigars should undergo through to detect potential diseases and further evaluate its health condition so that it can be prevented and treated as soon as possible.

For young Budgerigars, you might want to do a CBC or **Complete Blood Count**; this is a general test for birds and even humans to test for any internal infections. Another test is called **Chlamydophila Immunoassay**; this is a diagnosis exam to check if your bird might be carrying a contagious parrot fever, which is also potentially harmful to humans. You might also want to do a **Culture diagnosis** to detect if there are any bacterial infections in your young Budgerigars.

For adult Budgerigars, a CBC and Culture diagnosis should be done regularly as prescribed by your avian veterinarian as well as a full body X-ray usually with gas sedation for further evaluation of your pet's condition. If there are any signs of illness, veterinarians will recommend further tests to identify your bird's potential disease.

Signs of Possible Illnesses

For you to keep your Budgerigars healthy, you need to monitor them to ensure that they are in good condition, however there will come a time that your bird will get sick. Here are some early warning signs that your Budgerigars could be potentially ill.

- **Activity** – Is your bird sleeping when it normally does not? Or being quiet when it normally isn't? Is there a decreased in food and water intake or not being able to eat at all like before?
- **Droppings** (feces) - Are there any change in urates (white part) or feces that is lasting more than 1-2 days?
- **Diarrhea** - Have you found undigested food in your bird's feces? Their droppings should have the three distinct parts (green/brown, white and liquid urine). If you think your Budgerigars has diarrhea, contact your vet immediately.
- **Weight loss** - Does your bird feels "light" when you pick it up? That maybe a sign of weight loss because the Keel bone becomes more prominent.
- **Feathers** – Is there a continuous presence of pinfeathers? It may be dull in color, broken, bent and

fluffed up feathers.

- **Sneezing** – Is there a discharge in the nostrils when your bird sneezes? Look for stained feathers over the nares or crusty material in or around the nostrils.
- **Vomiting** – Has your pet been vomiting for quite a long period of time already? Budgerigars and all birds regurgitate occasionally as a sign of "affection" but it could also indicate a crop infection
- **Respiratory** – Are there signs of respiratory distress like tail bobbing up and down with each breath, a change in breathing sounds, and wheezing or clicking noise when it inhales?
- **Balance** – Has your bird been falling off its perch and huddling at the bottom of cage? It is a sign that it's losing its balance.
- **Eyes** – Does it appear dull? Is there a redness/swelling and loss of feathers around the eyes?
- **Feet** – Is it scaly or flaky? Does it have sores on the bottom of the feet?
- **Head** – Have you noticed excessive head bobbing and shaking?
- **Beak** – Is your bird's beak swelling?

- **Behavior** – does your bird sits on the floor of its cage or habitat? Does it favor one foot over the other?

When these things happen, contact your avian veterinarian immediately. Do not compromise your bird's health; prevention is always better than cure.

Chapter Eight: Budgerigar Checklist

Congratulate yourself! You are now on your way to becoming a very well-informed and pro-active Budgerigars owner! Finishing this book is a huge milestone for you and your future or present pet bird, but before this ultimate guide comes to a conclusion, keep in mind the most important things you have acquired through reading this book.

This chapter will outline the summary of what you have learned, the do's and dont's as well as the checklist you need to tick off to ensure that you and your Budgerigars lived happily ever after!

Basic Information

- Taxonomy: phylum *Chordata*, class *Aves*, order *Psittaciformes*, family *Psittaculidae*, Subfamily *Loriinae*, Tribe *Melopsittacini*
- **Distribution**: Australia
- **Habitat**: Scrublands, Woodlands, Grasslands
- **Lifestyle**: Flock Oriented
- **Anatomical Adaptations**:
- **Breeding Season**: between June to September
- **Eggs**: 4 – 6 eggs
- **Incubation Period**: 18 – 21 days
- **Sexual Maturity** : 6 – 7 months old
- **Average Size**: 18 cm (7 in)
- **Average Weight**: 30 – 40 grams
- **Wingspan**: 25 – 36 cm (10 – 14 in)
- **Coloration**: (in the wild) yellow, white, violet, gray, sky blue, cobalt, mauve; over 100 color mutations
- **Sexual Dimorphism**: Sexually dimorphic
- **Diet**: Seeds, Insects, Fruit, Nuts (Omnivore)
- **Sounds:** Vocal Communicator
- **Interaction:** Highly Social
- **Lifespan**: 15 – 20 years

Cage Set-up Guide

- **Minimum Cage Dimensions**: 24"x16"x16" (70x40x40cm)
- **Cage Shape**: the bigger, the better. Never purchase a round cage.
- **Bar Spacing**: not more than 0.5 in (1.3 cm)
- **Required Accessories**: food and water dishes, perches, grooming and cleaning materials, cuttlebone, toys
- **Food/Water Dish**: 3 sturdy dishes; one for fresh water, one for pellet/seed mix, and one for fresh foods. Do not buy dishes made out of plastic
- **Perches**: at least 3 different perches; wood dowel, natural branch type, a therapeutic perch or a cement perch or any fresh fruit tree branches
- **Recommended Toys**: rotate at least 3 different toys; rope toys, stainless steel bells, swings etc.
- **Bathing Materials**: misting bottle; bath tub
- **Nests Materials**: nest box made out of wood, oak or metal
- **Recommended Temperature Range**: 65-75°F (18 - 24°C)
- **Lighting:** full color light bulb must be present in the cage area. Do not use incandescent or monochromatic light bulbs.

Nutritional Information

- **Types of Recommended Food:**
- **Seeds:** 1/8 - 1/4 cup of fortified parrot seed mix
- **Fresh Fruits and Vegetables:** makes up about 15 to 20% of a Budgerigar's diet. Offer fruits and vegetables daily or every 2 - 3 days.
- **Supplements:** Calcium usually found in the form of a cuttlebone or Calcium treat. Powdered supplement such as packaged oyster shell can be added directly to your pet's food.
- **Amino Acids:** makes up about 20% of a Budgerigar's diet.
- **Carbohydrates:** makes up about 10% of a Budgerigar's diet (nuts, seeds, corn etc.)
- **Water:** clean, fresh and cool water; unflavored bottled drinking water or bottled natural spring water

Breeding Information

- **Sexual Dimorphism**: They are sexually dimorphic; gender can be identified through DNA sexing or chromosomal analysis.
- **Seasonal Changes**: breeding season usually begins in from June to September.
- **Sexual Maturity:** 6 months old

- **Nest Box Size:** 12"x12"x12" (30 x 30 x 30 cm)
- **Egg Laying:** female lays eggs an average of 4 – 6 eggs with an interval of 1 – 2 days.
- **Clutch Size:** about 4 - 6 clutches per year;
- **Incubation Period:** 18 – 21 days
- **Hatching:** takes about 24 – 48 hours to hatch
- **Chick Independence:** 1 – 2 months (50 - 60 days)

Do's and Dont's

- Do keep them busy and happy;
- Do feed them a variety of nutritious food
- Do train them well to maximize their intelligence
- Do provide a clean and healthy environment
- Do give them time and commitment
- Do care for them when they feel ill
- Do provide plenty of toys inside the cage
- Do bond with them and let them out of the cage once in a while so that they can be exposed outside
- Do not use sandpaper covered perches or floor paper. It can cause severe damage to your bird's feet
- Do not use "bird disks" or "mite disks". These may harm your bird. See your avian veterinarian if you suspect parasites.
- Do not use bird gravel. Bird gravel is used for birds that do not crack the hull or shell of the seeds they

eat. It causes severe impactions, which are often fatal. Gravel only benefits doves and pigeons definitely not parrots

- Do not use negative reinforcement during training because it is not effective
- Don't let Budgerigars fall. It may contribute in developing respiratory problems and damages organs due to impact. Train them how to fly instead!
- Do not let your Budgerigars get near to the following household items to prevent causes of accidents:

  - Ceiling or electric fans
  - Cooking oil
  - Leg chains
  - Toxic Fumes
  - Wood shavings
  - Toxic houseplants
  - Pesticides
  - Lead or zinc materials
  - Air fresheners
  - Scented candles
  - Sandpaper-covered perches
  - Tobacco and Cigarette smoke

Chapter Nine: Relevant Websites

Finishing this book doesn't mean that you should stop learning! This chapter provides you a wealth of references online that you could check out every now and then so that you can be updated when it comes to taking care of your Budgerigars. You can also find the websites you need to visit especially in buying cages and supplies for your pet.

Budgerigars Cage Links

Here is the recommended list of websites for you to choose from when buying cages both in United States and Great Britain.

United States Links:

Custom Cages
<https://www.customcages.com/catalogsearch/result/?o=Budgrigar+Cage&q=Budgie+right+Cage>

Bird Cages 4 Less
<http://birdcages4less.com/page/B/CTGY/Small_Bird_Cages>

Bird Cages Now
<http://www.birdcagesnow.com/budgies/>

Pet Solutions
<http://www.petsolutions.com/C/Bird-Cages-Carriers.aspx>

Pets at Home
<http://www.petsathome.com/shop/en/pets/bird-and-wildlife/bird-cages>

Overstock

<http://www.overstock.com/Pet-Supplies/Bird-Cages-Houses/3643/cat.html>

Great Britain Links:

Cages World

<http://www.cagesworld.co.uk/c/Budgie_Cages.htm>

Northern Parrots

<http://www.northernparrots.com/budgie-deptb103/?category=147>

Pebble – Home and Garden

<https://www.pebble.co.uk/compare.html?q=Budgerigars+cage>

Seapets

<https://www.seapets.co.uk/bird-supplies/bird-cages/parrot-cages>

Budgerigars Cage Accessories and Supplies

Here is the recommended list of websites for you to choose from when buying accessories such as toys, perches, dishes and other necessary supplies for your pet.

United States Links:

King's Cages

<http://www.kingscages.com/ >

Doctors Foster and Smith – Toys

<http://www.drsfostersmith.com/bird-supplies/ >

Fun Time Birdy - Toys

<http://www.funtimebirdy.com/patoyse.html>

Pet Mountain – Cleaning Supplies

< http://www.petmountain.com/category/311/1/bird-cage-cleaning-supplies.html>

PetSmart – Bowls, Feeders

<http://www.petsmart.com/bird/bowls-feeders/cat-36-catid-400014>

Wind City Parrot - Accessories
<http://www.windycityparrot.com/All_c_711.html>

Pet Solutions - Breeding Supplies
<http://www.petsolutions.com/C/Bird-Breeding-Supplies.aspx>

Bird Cages 4 Less - Perches
<http://birdcages4less.com/page/B/CTGY/Bird_Perches>

Pets at Home – Health Care Products
<http://www.petsathome.com/shop/en/pets/bird-and-wildlife/bird-healthcare-products>

Overstock - Accessories
<http://www.overstock.com/Pet-Supplies/Bird-Accessories/3646/cat.html>

Great Britain Links:

Cages World - Accessories
<http://www.cagesworld.co.uk/c/Bird_Cage_Accessories.htm>

Parrot Essentials - Accessories

<http://www.parrotessentials.co.uk/>

Parrotize UK – Parrot Stands and Covers

<http://parrotize.co.uk/products/parrot-stands/>

Seapets – Bird Toys

<https://www.seapets.co.uk/bird-supplies/bird-toys>

ZooPlus – Accessories
<http://www.zooplus.co.uk/shop/birds/cage_accessories>

Budgerigars Diet and Food Links

Here is the recommended list of websites for you to choose from when buying seeds and parrot food for your pet.

United States Links:

Pet Mountain
<http://www.petmountain.com/category/314/1/Budgerigars-food.html>

Harrison's Bird Food

<http://www.harrisonsbirdfoods.com/>

Nature Chest - Bird Food

<http://www.naturechest.com/bifoforinri.html>

Petco – Bird Food; Treats

<http://www.petco.com/shop/en/petcostore/bird/bird-food-and-treats>

Pet Supplies Plus

<http://www.petsuppliesplus.com/thumbnail/Bird/Food-Treats/c/2142/2162.uts>

That Pet Place – Bird Food Supplies

<http://www.thatpetplace.com/bird-supplies/bird-food#!bird-food>

Great Britain Links:

Parrot Essentials UK – Vitamins and Minerals for birds

<http://www.parrotessentials.co.uk/vitamins-minerals/>

Scarletts Parrot Essentials UK – Bird Food

<http://www.scarlettsparrotessentials.co.uk/food>

Seapets – Bird Food

<https://www.seapets.co.uk/bird-supplies/bird-food/bird-seeds>

ZooPlus

<http://www.zooplus.co.uk/shop/birds/bird_food/parrot>

Bird Food UK

<http://www.birdfood.co.uk/ctrl/node:114;page:2;/bird_food s>

Ideal Price UK

<http://www.idealprice.co.uk/compare.html?q=Budgerigars %20food>

Northern Parrots – Parrot Treatments

<http://www.northernparrots.com/treatments-and-cures-dept139/>

Index

A

B

C

D

Photo Credits

Page 1 Photo by user JamesDeMers via Pixabay.com, <https://pixabay.com/en/blue-parakeet-bird-blue-parrot-204698/>

Page 12 Photo by user Kakaket via Pixabay.com, <https://pixabay.com/en/birds-budgerigars-together-645810/>

Page 13 Photo by user Marie Hale via Pixabay.com, <https://www.flickr.com/photos/15016964@N02/6293980869/>

Page 26 Photo by user Osio via Flickr.com, <https://www.flickr.com/photos/osio/2541615442/in/photolist>

Page 28 Photo by user Harsha K R via Wikimedia Commons, <https://commons.wikimedia.org/wiki/Budgerigars#/media/File:Budgerigars_and_Cockatiel.jpg>

Page 36 Photo by user Axe77 via Pixabay.com, <https://pixabay.com/en/bird-budgie-budgerigar-parakeet-677195/>

Page 39 Photo by user Osio via Flickr.com,
<https://www.flickr.com/photos/osio/2111919582/in/photolis
t>

Page 53 Photo by user NellyBelly via Pixabay.com,
<https://pixabay.com/en/birds-budgerigars-animals-feather-
1039132/>

Page 62 Photo by user Budgme via Pixabay.com,
<https://pixabay.com/en/bird-parrot-animal-pet-small-
616873/>

Page 78 Photo by user Cocoparisienne via Pixabay.com,
<https://pixabay.com/en/budgerigars-birds-parakeets-
animal-331834/>

Page 94Photo by user Osio via Flickr.com,
<https://www.flickr.com/photos/osio/2111986998/in/photolis
t>

Page 114 Photo by user Hibaby via Wikimedia Commons,
<https://commons.wikimedia.org/wiki/File:Budgerigar.JPG>

Page 121 Photo by user InspiredImages via Pixabay.com,
<https://pixabay.com/en/bird-budgie-pet-parrot-budgerigar-
1259286/>

References

"10 Most Common Budgie Diseases" Petplace.com
<http://www.petplace.com/article/birds/general/when-your-bird-is-sick/10-most-common-budgie-diseases>

"Bringing Pet Birds into UK" Jamescargo.com
<http://www.jamescargo.com/livestock_transport/PetBirdImport.htm>

"Budgerigar" A-Zanimals.com
<http://a-z-animals.com/animals/budgerigar/>

"Budgerigar" NewWorldEncyclopedia.com
<http://www.newworldencyclopedia.org/entry/Budgerigar>

"Budgerigar aka Budgie" BeautyofBirds.com
<https://www.beautyofbirds.com/budgieinfo.htm>

"Budgerigars/Budgie – Common Diseases"
BeautyofBirds.com
<https://www.beautyofbirds.com/budgiediseases.html>

"Budgerigar, Parakeets" Animal-World.com
<http://animal-world.com/encyclo/birds/parakeets/budgies.php>

"Mutations and Genetics" Ibudgie.com

<https://ibudgie.wordpress.com/mutations-and-genetics/>

"The Beauty of Budgerigar: Colors, Mutations and More" Budgerigar.com

<http://www.budgerigar.com/books/the-beauty-of-the-budgeriga.html>

UK Breeders Listings

<http://www.preloved.co.uk/>

USA Breeders Listings

<http://www.birdbreeders.com/>

Feeding Baby
Cynthia Cherry
978-1941070000

Axolotl
Lolly Brown
978-0989658430

Dysautonomia, POTS
Syndrome
Frederick Earlstein
978-0989658485

Degenerative Disc
Disease Explained
Frederick Earlstein
978-0989658485

Sinusitis, Hay Fever,
Allergic Rhinitis Explained
Frederick Earlstein
978-1941070024

Wicca
Riley Star
978-1941070130

Zombie Apocalypse
Rex Cutty
978-1941070154

Capybara
Lolly Brown
978-1941070062

Eels As Pets
Lolly Brown
978-1941070167

Scabies and Lice Explained
Frederick Earlstein
978-1941070017

Saltwater Fish As Pets
Lolly Brown
978-0989658461

Torticollis Explained
Frederick Earlstein
978-1941070055

Kennel Cough
Lolly Brown
978-0989658409

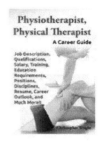

Physiotherapist, Physical
Therapist
Christopher Wright
978-0989658492

Rats, Mice, and Dormice
As Pets
Lolly Brown
978-1941070079

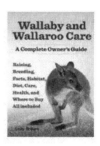

Wallaby and Wallaroo Care
Lolly Brown
978-1941070031

Bodybuilding Supplements
Explained
Jon Shelton
978-1941070239

Demonology
Riley Star
978-19401070314

Pigeon Racing
Lolly Brown
978-1941070307

Dwarf Hamster
Lolly Brown
978-1941070390

Cryptozoology
Rex Cutty
978-1941070406

Eye Strain
Frederick Earlstein
978-1941070369

Inez The Miniature Elephant
Asher Ray
978-1941070353

Vampire Apocalypse
Rex Cutty
978-1941070321

Made in the USA
Monee, IL
12 June 2023

35678001R00083